'When Helen was a little girl I remember her writing stories for her brother and sisters and even then the imagination and quality of the tales was obvious.

These stories are enough to make you laugh out loud even on a crowded train, which can be embarrassing. The first time I read them I could not stop laughing (a tears of laughter job) As I worked on the illustrations and reread each story carefully, I laughed again and again even though I had been over exposed to them.

This little book will brighten your day.

How much is laughter worth? Answer a lot more than the price of this hilarious book' - Graeme Sims

'What do I like about this book? Well, it makes me laugh, because the stories are funny and well written (consider that English is not my first language).

The peculiarity is also that they are true anecdotes and this makes them even more remarkable.

Finally, I love that they have animals involved and that they are never the "strange" part of the stories, while humans often are' - Valentina Teghillo

Pampered Pets Outrageous Owners

Pampered Pets Outrageous Owners

Illustrations by Graeme Sims

Helen Brunton

I would like to dedicate this book to my first beagle called Binky. She was the most naughty but clever dog I have ever had. We brought her home when she was a puppy of 10 weeks old.

She quickly learned how to steal food and even open cupboards. When my husband Bill was putting up a long fence to keep her in our garden, she was looking at him through the new fence from the other side! So that plan didn't work at first then. She would climb up our hedge as agile as a cat. She would watch and work it all out for herself.

So when I say beagles have an overdose of character, it is Binky I am always thinking about!

Contents

Acknowledgements

I would like to say a big thank you to my husband Bill who read through my manuscript more than once to give me feedback and help with suggestions for the characters.

I would like to thank my daughter, Kirsty who helped me by reading my manuscript and helping me with editing it.

I would also like to thank my Dad, Graeme Sims and Valentina Teghillo who brought my book to life and made it possible to have it published for me. Dad, thank you for the great illustrations – which covered everything exactly as I had written it.

I also thank all the above for ongoing encouragement with writing this book.

Preface

I t all started when my daughter began to look after local peoples' cats and dogs in the village where we live. It was a great idea for her to earn some pocket money while she was at college. My daughter printed off some flyers and we set off to deliver them to every house in our village. Within a couple of days we had people phoning to ask if we could help with their pets. To start with it was mainly for cat feeding.

I had always been involved with different sorts of animals. We kept chickens, ducks, rabbits, dogs and cats. When I was 11 years old one Christmas, I was lying in bed wide awake waiting for Santa to come. I must have started to doze off when I heard the sound of hooves go past my window. I looked out but of course there was nothing there.

The next morning was Christmas Day. I got up to go to breakfast and open my presents. I had some toys and dolls and the normal sort of stuff a girl of my age would like. After breakfast, my dad told me there was one more present waiting for me to see. At the end of our garden there was a stable which had been there for years and it was never used.

Today was different. Today there was a little grey donkey in there looking out the window at me! My dad had rescued her. She had been a beach donkey giving rides to children and then got too old to do a day's work and was therefore no longer needed.

I had never ridden before and so started to learn with this donkey. She became my best friend and I would spend hours with her. I loved her melting chocolate intelligent eyes and soft muzzle. We started off with walking up and down my road. The fastest she would go was in a brisk trot but that was fast enough for me. I soon learned how to ride in a trot and get the rhythm right!

In those days there was no such thing as Health and Safety and I would jump up onto the donkey's back with no hard hat or proper boots. I would ride her with no saddle and just a lead rope round her neck and often I would just have my flip flops on. But I never ever fell off her luckily. She was too gentle to let me fall off. I called her Tessa and would ride her up and down the hill we lived on to go and see my friends. Instead of a bike, I had a donkey. My friends' families never minded me tying Tessa up on their lawns while I went in to have tea with them. My friends' parents would come home and say to me that they knew

I was here as Tessa was parked on their lawn. Tessa didn't mind as she was very sweet natured and she would be given a couple of cakes and some fruit. We also had chickens, ducks and rabbits and I grew up with various dogs and animals which has probably helped me a great deal in doing this job and looking after other peoples' pets – and their owners a lot of the time!

I started working at a large law firm in the City as a temp secretary for 2 days. I was then offered a permanent position which I accepted and that lasted 31 years. I was used to working to tight deadlines, long hours and in very modern plush surroundings. There were glass lifts and lots of marble and steel. Everything had to be done very precisely of course as there were lots of big, well known clients and lots of even bigger well-known deals going on. It was perfectly normal to be asked to work late and then carry on through the night. I got used to this exciting and manic way of life.

Sometimes in a quieter moment between the extremely busy atmosphere of the City, I would look out the window and think how nice it would be not to always have deadlines to work to and indeed, not to have to travel up to London on the train every day.

Country Life

My firm were looking at offering voluntary redundancy. I was away on holiday when the letter came through so had it waiting for me on my return. It seemed like fate to me as my daughter had just left college and was looking for a full-time job. This meant that she would now not be able to keep her business running.

I offered to keep the customers for her and then if ever she needed to come back to pet sitting, she could have the jobs back which would keep all her customers happy. What I didn't realise at the time was that I was to meet some characters who certainly gave a new meaning to Pets and Sitting! In effect I swapped glass for grass and steel for fields. I had nobody giving me deadlines – the dogs didn't mind if I went over their walk time by five minutes and nor did their owners. The cats I sat with were perfectly happy to sit and watch TV with me and purred away just to have some company and to watch Judge Rinder during the day. It didn't take long to get used to this slower pace of life and I found I really enjoyed it and looked forward to seeing my animal clients as much as they did me. To walk across a field to get to my cat clients first thing in the morning when the sun was coming up was a very content and calming experience for me. No trains, no crowds and no stress.

Nightie Night

I had a man called Jason phone me - he had got my details from the village magazine where I would put an advertisement and had a black cat called Betty who meant the world to him so he was very fussy about who would look after her whilst he was away for a week on business. He kept telling me that he couldn't stand it if anything happened to Betty - so this made me a bit paranoid from the start. I arranged to visit Betty and Jason - her besotted owner. Betty needed medication three times a day and unless you have tried to give a cat tablets you wouldn't know what an impossible and dodgy thing this is to do. Jason said that if I couldn't get a tablet down Betty's throat, I could always ring his vet who charged a lot to come out and perform this difficult task but Jason didn't care how much he spent on his precious cat. I arrived at Jason's large Edwardian house. My shoes crunched over the expensive gravel of the circular drive. It was very spacious and there were lots of different rooms. I was thinking I would need a map to find the cat!

Jason told me that Betty was upstairs in his bedroom and I was to go up. He followed me closely and I was having my doubts about this by then.

He introduced me to Betty who was reclining on his big double bed with cream silk sheets. I thought then this was a bad move for me to be up here just with him and Betty. Jason had a tablet in his hand and he asked that I stretch across the bed and give it to the cat. He said he had some minced chicken that was her favourite and rolled the tablet in the chicken. I said he could do it and I would watch. The cat duly opened her mouth daintily and let him push the pill down her throat. She showed her teeth but didn't use them. I was feeling uneasy being upstairs in Jason's bedroom I then walked back down the stairs at a brisk pace. Jason had asked that I take the job on and he would pay me next time as he hadn't had time to go to the cash point. He asked if we could just "hang out" and he would pay me for my time. I was old enough to be Jason's mother but he wasn't worried about that. He asked if I had an item of clothing that I could drop by for Betty so she could get used to my scent, and therefore feel more comfortable with me to take her tablets. I had an old nightie which I left in a carrier bag on the front door step to Jason's house next time I was passing. That night I got a picture message from Jason - he was sitting in bed wearing my nightie!! The next day I rang him to say that I would not be taking the job on and he could keep the nightie!

Cat Napping

My very first job was for an elderly couple and their equally elderly black cat. The cat, Meg, was in her 20s which was always a bit of a worry for me - would she last whilst they were away? Would she be okay on her own between visits? Where would she be when I came to see her? Most of the time she would be asleep anyway, so as long as I left her food out, she would be okay. As this was my first job, I wanted it to go well.

Luckily Meg was always asleep on a comfy chair upstairs in the study. I would go to see her and call her name, but she didn't wake up as she was deaf. So, then I would carefully tiptoe across the room to make sure she was still breathing - and she was each time – so that was a huge relief for me.

When the couple came home, I would go to see them to give the key back and collect my money. The lady loved to talk to me and kept asking me questions. I had quite a nice chat with her. Not so, her husband. He was pleasant enough but definitely not a talker. He would leave the front door open and point up to the sky and say "Well Helen, there is a big black cloud coming over. If you leave now you can get to your car without getting wet! He would then offer me an umbrella so I could be on my way. I would start to edge towards the door - only for his wife to start another conversation! Do I stay, Do I go? I hovered in the doorway still talking to his wife. The husband then got very fidgety and again told me about the big black cloud. I then decided it was time to go, carrying on my conversation with the wife until I got to my car door.

Doggy steps...

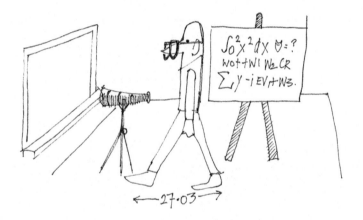

I had a customer – I will call him Mr Precise, who wanted to record every walk I took his dog on. Mr Precise lived alone and used to be a maths teacher so he loved spreadsheets and charts. I had to go for an interview to meet his dog – which was a little black cocker spaniel called Ellie. Ellie was very calm and laid back so it made a good contrast to her pent-up owner. I went up to meet Mr. Precise one afternoon and luckily for me I was bang on time. I was invited in for tea and to see his dog. I asked how many walks were needed and was told 3 a week. Mr. Precise got out a large piece of paper and asked me to sign in and out for each walk, note the weather and how many times Ellie stopped for a wee whilst I was out.

That's fine I thought, cocker spaniels are usually good easy dogs who are quite attentive and well behaved, so I won't have any trouble with my time keeping in getting her back to him as Ellie was well trained and didn't seem the type to run off for a long time from my first impression of her.

I agreed to start the next day. I went to pick up Ellie and she jumped in the back of my car good as gold. When I got back from the walk I was asked where we had been. I explained we had been to the forest which had taken me exactly an hour. Mr. Precise asked me how many steps we had done! I don't wear a pedometer so had no idea but guessed. Not good enough! We have to know how many steps we are taking so Mr. Precise knows he is getting good value. He even had printed off a spreadsheet so he could plot the steps for next time.

I told him I didn't use a pedometer but if his dog had a good hour's exercise and came back happy wasn't that the most important thing? No, next time Ellie would have a pedometer attached to her collar so I couldn't cheat his system. This customer lasted for a month and by that time I had had enough of studying spreadsheets and counting steps. I hated maths when I was at school so did not want to be doing this every time. It was a shame as Ellie was an easy little dog to take out. She was five years old and very fit and she loved her walks with me, as I did her. If it wasn't for her owner, we could have walked miles every week –but for me it was just a step too far.

Something is afoot

I took on a job for a retired chiropodist. He was great fun and told me lots of stories. He had a hamster that he wanted "sitting". I am not sure how you "sit" a hamster or even if they are that interested in someone being in the same room as them. But it seemed a nice job so I went to visit little Hammy three times a week. Hammy was not demanding and mostly asleep when I went to see him.

Hammy's owner, Ricky was so funny. He told me how he would have patients come to his surgery to have the hard skin on their feet removed. He would keep this hard skin in a jar and when his mother in law came to visit, he would mix the hard skin with some parmesan cheese and just let her "sprinkle away" when he served her favourite spag bol. He always felt happier when she left as he felt he had "paid her back" for all the hard times and sharp words she had given him in the past. She often said that she loved his spag bol and it had a certain "something" to it that she couldn't quite put her finger on! It most certainly did.

The job with Hammy went on for a year - but Hammy bit me one day when I came to visit him. Ricky had left me a note to clean out Hammy and feed him. I usually just had to look at him in his bed made of hay just to make sure he was still alive. Anyway, armed with some fresh hay and sawdust, I looked in the bedroom compartment and saw Hammy was sleeping. I gently put my hand in to stroke him and tried not to startle him. So far so good. I had him in the palm of my hand and was just transferring him to a small box so I could clean his cage out. I felt a sharp nip on my finger and had to let go of him. Hammy scampered away and ran up the chimney. I had no way of getting him back and put my arm up into the fireplace to try to reach him which didn't work. I was thinking of buying another hamster to put in the cage so nobody noticed but Hammy was a white hamster - and at the time they were not easily available to buy. So, the original Hammy must have gone to the big wheel in the sky and wasn't replaced as Ricky went to live in France. I went home covered in soot from the chimney with my finger bleeding from his sharp little teeth. It took me ages to get my hair back to its normal light brown colour rather than black from the soot.

Not like Harry Potter!

A few years ago, my dad found a baby tawny owl. He kept an eye on it but the mother did not come back. So, he brought it in the house and kept it in a dis-used aviary in the garden. The baby got stronger and grew quite friendly towards us. We called him Sage and he wanted lots of attention. He would come into the lounge while we watched TV in the evening.

Sage would sit on the curtain poles and look at us to see if anybody would give him attention. If we ignored him, he would swoop down from the curtain poles and with his claws, catch each one of us on the head and lightly rake through our hair on his way by. He would then fly up to the opposite end of the room and screech loudly. He was very friendly and would lie on his back on my lap with his eyes shut relaxing. He had the most beautiful blue eye lids and would be quite relaxed in that position for ages.

Eventually when he got bigger, he would live outside in the apple tree, always returning at night to be fed so we would let him in. He stayed with us for a long time until one morning he just left. I would not want him to deliver my mail – I think he would throw it at me!

New Year's Eve - a rabbit's tale

A lady called Emma who I had known for a while, had a large black lop-eared rabbit who had a very different way of celebrating New Year's Eve. He just loved to eat electrical wires and had already ruined her Dyson vacuum cleaner twice by biting and chewing the flex. Luckily the electrical system was earth protected so he couldn't get a shock. We called him Mr. Dyson because of this. He loved all the lights that were sparkling away on the tree and around the house. He especially loved to chew the wires of the lights!

When Emma went away and I looked after Mr. Dyson, I had to go into every room in the house and turn off all the lights at the socket so if he did fancy a little nibble at midnight, he would not come to any harm. Emma insisted that the rabbit would be allowed to celebrate on New Year's Eve and asked that I would put a party hat on his head with elastic under his chin, and send her a photo. When midnight came and there were fireworks on TV, he would get very agitated and start to run around the house looking for wires to eat! He also had a love of ginger biscuits. I decided that a plate of ginger nuts would be a brighter idea than electric wires so this would be his new treat every year. For living dangerously, he really took the biscuit!

Never trust a ferret!

I had a phone call one morning from Patience, a lady who lived at the end of our road to ask if I would be available to look after a ferret. Patience called me and asked if I could go to Norfolk with her as they would be selling ferrets at a country fair that she went to every year. I thought it would be a bit of fun and a day out so off we went. Patience was a very posh lady and she liked everything in its place and neat and tidy.

She was the sort of person who would go round the house with an air freshener all day as her house smelt like a perfume factory. She would often hold a posh afternoon tea for her friends who were ladies she had met at the local golf club. The competition to have a new set of clubs, carpet or car was fierce with the other ladies. Even a new pet would start off their competitive natures.

I had not handled ferrets since I was a little girl and had forgotten how smelly they were! I hoped I would remember how to handle them.

Patience said it would be a novelty to have a ferret and she might be able to outdo the golf club ladies when they did their usual show and tell. The ladies always had exotic new pets to show off about.

There was an old man at the country show and he had a barrel which was on its side full of baby ferrets all running around and chasing each other. Patience chose a young brown and cream male ferret who she called Tiggy.

We took her new addition "Tiggy" home and made him a house in an old empty rabbit hutch at the end of her garden. There was a very musky smell to Tiggy but I thought as he was outside it wouldn't be a problem.

Patience soon decided Tiggy could stay with me for a few weeks - I think the smell of him got the better of her. She asked if I could please bring him round to show to her ladies who lunch - but then take him back to my place as he was a bit "pungent".

While he was young - Tiggy was a sweet and amusing pet. He would hold on to my finger without biting it and liked to sit on my lap. How things were to change!

A few weeks later Patience was to hold her afternoon tea. The six ladies came to her house to visit. She told them about Tiggy and the ladies seemed impressed as they had never been up close to a ferret before and asked if they could hold him. I went to collect him from his hutch and gave him to Patience, she thought he was lovely and he started to climb up and lick her ear lobe. Tiggy was on his best behaviour!

Another lady from the golf club was Annabelle. Annabelle had a little pug that she brought to the afternoon tea. Puggy was very loud and snored and snorted all the time. He would sit under the table while his owner showed off about his wonderful pedigree and passed around photos of his puppyhood. There were photos of every stage of Puggy's life for each week, so this took a long while to get through. Annabelle would pass little tid bits to Puggy which was useful as she was always on a strict diet and didn't eat most of what she put on her plate. Puggy would gratefully take any morsel he was given. Annabelle colour co-ordinated all her outfits to match Puggy. Today she was sporting a light beige cashmere cardigan with a brown skirt and a beautiful Radley handbag of the same colour. Puggy had his Burberry bow tie on in beige and brown and they looked a picture. It just so happened that Tiggy was the colour of Puggy too. How nice for everything to match in. Annabelle had recently had surgery around her eyes and she looked surprised all the time. Her eyes seemed to bulge out like Puggy's so she told everyone they were related.

Patience had also invited her sister, Faith, who looked very thin and brittle as if she might break. She was a tiny bird like woman and had to have a cushion on her chair so she could reach the dining table. Faith would not be outdone by Patience and so wanted to hold the ferret too - to show the other ladies that she could do everything her older sister could and that she too was good with animals. Patience and Faith didn't really get on at all but both would not be outdone by the other. Faith picked up a dainty sandwich filled with juicy ham. The sandwich was quite heavy for her little hand but she would never admit that. She offered Tiggy the juicy ham from her sandwich. Happy to be invited to the afternoon tea as he wasn't usually allowed in buildings because of his scent, he licked his lips, bared his teeth and happily dug in. But the taste of the ham had given him a craving for more meat.

I went into the kitchen to ask if Patience needed any help with the lunch. I was just about to pick up a plate of sandwiches when I heard a piercing shriek!! Rushing out to see what had happened, I was greeted with Faith running around the room with her hands in the air and Tiggy locked on to her ear by his sharp little teeth! Ferrets can lock their jaws and so the last thing you must do is try to pull them off. Tiggy was locked on for a good few minutes and the screaming was only making him worse. The only way to release Faith's ear from Tiggy's teeth, was to bring a piece of chicken to tempt Tiggy to release his jaw. Luckily, he had finished his ham and decided chicken would be a nice change. As we were having dainty chicken sandwiches too, this worked out very well. He preferred chicken to a scrawny guest's ear or a piece of ham. The ladies were quite worn out with all this going on. Faith needed a large gin as she had one of her headaches coming on and then had to have a lie down on the sofa. Annabelle picked up Puggy (who was getting quite heavy by this time and all the extra food he had eaten, and struggled out to put him in her car and take him home where he would probably need a lie down too!

I managed to get Tiggy back into his hutch but that day Patience lost her Faith and we all lost our Patience, which wasn't a bad thing as she never came round again to ask me favours and I didn't have to listen to the golf ladies boasting about their exotic pets! I thought that a gin for me too wasn't a bad idea after all the excitement.

Look what the cat
brought in...

I had a lovely regular job looking after a big ginger tom cat. He was as big as a corgi and loved lots of fuss. I used to go round to see Ginger Tom twice a day to feed him. He was always waiting for me to arrive and the minute I called him, he would appear from nowhere and beat me to the front door.

Tom would always bring me in little treats and I had to go round the whole house checking the rooms to make sure he hadn't left me anything. One day I arrived to see Tom to find there was a pheasant stuck in the cat flap. I moved Tom out of the way so I could have a better look. As I touched its wing, it started shrieking and trying to flap its wing that wasn't stuck. It gave me a shock and Tom was suddenly interested again. I had to get it out before the owners came back. I pulled it and pushed it and it wouldn't move. I also had to put Tom back outside as he was very proud of his catch and wanted to get involved with me pulling it out. I gradually inched the pheasant out of the cat flap and suddenly it was free and very upset. The doors to the upstairs floor had not been shut and off went the pheasant trying to walk and fly at the same time. All the upstairs bedroom doors were still open too so I had to shoo it out of each room and close each door as I went.

I decided to let it calm down a bit and I went off to make myself a cup of tea. After 15 minutes the bird had calmed down. I managed to coax it into the bathroom and throw a towel over it. It stopped squawking and seemed to have given up. I took it downstairs and across the road to a quiet field. I had locked Tom in his house so he couldn't follow me. As I unwrapped the towel, the pheasant squawked and flew away. I was so happy to see him go. The next day I went back to see Tom. I also found a few little voles and mice that he had hidden under the sofa. I didn't get much relaxation with Tom but after I had cleared away all his "presents", he would come and sit on my lap and be as sweet as a little kitten and would always fall asleep after all his hunting.

Basic training

I had an email from a man in the village who said he was called Yorkie. At first, I thought he probably came from Yorkshire so the name must have stayed with him. He said he wanted some basic training sessions and was I able to dish out some discipline for a naughty dog. I said that I really either visited animals and walked them but if his dog was a puppy then I could certainly be help him out with some basics. He said that this dog was a puppy and any attention I could give it would be good. I made an appointment to go and see him the following afternoon. He had just bought a big house in the village and I knew the area well, which was just up the road from me.

I set off in good time. I had to announce myself at the entry phone next to the big black electric gates. There was a big sign up saying – wait for the bark then state your business and your name. There was no bark and Yorkie didn't answer so I gave it a few minutes and then tried to phone him. Still no answer, so I thought I might as well drive home and wait for him to contact me.

I got a phone call from him an hour later - saying sorry that he hadn't been there and that if

I came up to see him now, he would be there and would open the gates for me.

I drove up to the black gates again and this time there was a bark. I announced that I had arrived and who I was, and in slow motion the large black wrought iron gates opened for me. Yorkie came to open my car door for me and showed me into the kitchen of his beautiful house. The house was big and the rooms were like something from a property magazine.

I was offered a seat at the table where there was a large collar, a lead and a plate of dog biscuits left out on the kitchen counter. I asked him if he had come down from York to have the name "Yorkie" and he said not but it was his breed! Alarm bells did ring but I just thought he had a sense of humour.

I was offered coffee or water (which I refused and a dog biscuit which I also refused) as I just wanted to get on with the job and I was already an hour behind schedule for getting to my other jobs that day. Yorkie sat there picking up a dog biscuit and then choosing another one and putting that back on the plate. He told me he was a fussy eater and tried not to feed between meals. He offered me a doggie bag to put some biscuits in and take home with me. He picked up a dog brush and asked if I would like to do some grooming. Again, I declined his offer. This was getting stranger by the minute.

Time was ticking on and still no mention of his dog nor any sign of what training he wanted for his dog. I asked to see his dog as I had other appointments to go to after him.

Yorkie said he would go and see where the bad dog had got to. I sat in the kitchen watching the big clock, waiting. Time was ticking by.

All of a sudden, the kitchen door banged open and Yorkie came bounding into the kitchen wearing a fur coat and a pair of boxer shorts and a collar and lead and sat on the floor panting at me! It was so funny - but very worrying at the same time. I did not know where to look and whether to laugh or scream. He told me he had been a bad dog for not being there to greet me and needed a spanking and then to be taken out for a walk and then a bath! I said I had an emergency to go to and I told him to go to his bed and STAY! He went straight to his large dog bed and sat down. I threw him a dog biscuit Not surprisingly;

I didn't return to release him from his STAY - so by now he might hopefully have learned some basics!

Thirst Class horse

I am listed in the local magazine as a pet sitter - but I have also looked after horses. I used to ride a long while ago, and had my own horse so I have experience of horses. My beautiful client this time was a chestnut gelding called Barney. He was owned by a snooty lady called Gabriella - but Gabby to her public. Gabby regularly took Barney to show jumping events. She would ask me to go with her as she thought I had a calming influence on Barney and would keep him settled whilst he waited in the horsebox for his turn in the show jumping ring. Gabby loved to make an entrance and always timed it perfectly to enter the ring.

Gabby was very glamorous with a long blonde plait, jet black eyeliner and scarlet lipstick always in place. She always looked immaculate and so did her horse Barney Rubble.

We set off at dawn to go to a big show. Barney was in the horsebox so I had a chat about the weather to him. When we arrived at the event, Gabby went off to socialise and show off to her adoring public. On this particular event, she knew the local paper would be covering the show jumping and had made herself more beautiful than ever as she was hoping for a front-page photo. She knew she outshone all the other women who were more interested in getting their horses groomed. Well, Gabby had me to groom the horse and so she could spend more time on herself. After all, the camera does not lie and it would not be good to have an unflattering photo. So, turned out in her cream jodhpurs and smart black jacket, she looked a picture and was walking round to chat to all the other women and give a dazzling white smile to all the men. Gabby was in her element.

I stayed with Barney and chatted as I groomed him. I drank my diet coke and coffee to keep me awake. While my back was turned, he pushed off the lid of the plastic cool box, pulled out a can of diet coke and bit through it. The can exploded, sending fizzy drink everywhere. To my amazement, he wouldn't let go of the can until it was empty. Luckily, none of the judges walked around but stayed near the show jumping ring, so nobody saw his bubbles!

I finished grooming Barney and went off to finish my can of diet coke. I couldn't find it so I thought I would go and get another can from the cool box.

Gabby had a brilliant - if not faster than ever before round - and I have never seen Barney jump so well and so high! Gabby didn't look so perfectly turned out at the end of the round, and the paparazzi were on hand to take plenty of photos of her not looking quite so perfect - but she did come first!

Dog wins cinema tickets

I worked for a lady called Iris who was very eccentric. She was in her 40s and would regularly enter competitions in her local paper. She would also put an entry in for her dog Lucy, who was a black Labrador, so her pen name was Lucy Black. One day Iris got a phone call from the local paper saying that Miss Lucy Black had won tickets to the local cinema for a colouring competition. Lucy Black was told to phone the local paper in order to be presented with her tickets. Iris rang the cinema to tell them that her dog had won tickets. She was asked to bring her dog along so they would have a photo taken and be presented with the prize.

Iris asked if I would take Lucy along with her for a bit of moral support.

When we got to the cinema, the manager presented the lucky Labrador with a big bag of dog food and Iris with the cinema tickets and a big bag of pick and mix sweets, drinks and ice cream Iris was more than happy not to have her picture taken with Lucy Black. The Labrador became quite famous for entering the competition.

Do you feel lucky pig?
Well do you?

I had a job where I had to look after three large pigs – called "Good", "Bad" and "Ugly". The pigs were really greedy and always heard me arriving – they recognised my car. I couldn't help thinking of the Clint Eastwood films – especially with the pigs having those names.

For a bit of fun I would lurk behind the straw bales and surprise them.

I would then emerge – with a tray full of bananas calling "Well, pig do you feel lucky"? whilst they were rooting around with their backs to me. I would then pounce and the bananas would fly through the air thick and fast! Anybody watching would have thought I was absolutely mad!

The pigs would push each other and squeal loudly. I would stand on the straw bales and watch them. The bananas had been stored in boxes in a hot tin shed for a couple of weeks so were by this time, a sticky mess. After the gun battle (with bananas), I asked "Do you feel lucky? Did I fire 5 or 6 bananas? In all this confusion, I can't remember – but do you feel lucky PIG? Well do you?" I would tip the remaining whole lot in the pig pen and it would be gone in seconds.

After 5 minutes or so peace was restored. The pigs were worn out from the feeding frenzy and I could return before High Noon".

Show Time

Once a year I would go to our local village dog show. I would see my regular customers there and hand our flyers for my dog walking and pet sitting. It was good to have a chance to talk to my customers as they were usually out working when I went to see their pets. I would always meet new customers too and as their dogs were with them at the show, it would give me the chance to see how the dogs behaved and if they would be good to look after or walk or a nightmare.

I had a customer called Stacey or Stace to all her close friends. Stace had the most beautiful red setter called Merlot. Stace was very proud of her beautiful dog and had coloured her own hair to match the vibrant mahogany colour of her dog Merlot. Stace always wore sugar pink clothes from head to foot. Her dog wore pink too so they always matched each other. They were always pretty in pink.

Stace had very long pink nails too and her dog had pink nails but not quite so long.

It was always "my Merlot". Stace had dazzling white teeth and loved a sunbed. She even tried to get her skin the colour of her dog too which meant many hours of sunbeds and spray tans. She had lip fillers and lots of other fillers all over. The male judges flirted with her and Stace would be happy thinking that her Merlot had a chance. "Well gel" she would say to me – if the judges notice me they will notice my Merlot and she might get a good place". Stace hated it when it was a woman judge as she thought the women judges were jealous of her and she had to work harder with them. "They certainly won't get best in show" Stace would tell everyone.

But if it was a man judge – well she would be made up. The men judges would often come over to see her dog a few times more than they needed and would insist on smiling at the beautiful Merlot and her attractive owner. They would particularly like to see Stace move around the ring!

This particular time, Stace rang me and said she had broken her toe and would I be able to show her Merlot for her the at the Annual Village Show. I had helped Stace out before when she took Merlot to different shows as Stace often had a bit of trouble with her toes and couldn't always walk or run at a decent pace to show her dog off to the judge. The trouble with her toes was the shoes she wore. Glittery pink platforms which nobody would be able to run round in. She liked me as I wore trainers so there was no competition with her glamorous shoes.

The show was held in a massive barn which was divided into 8 show rings.

"Good luck darlin" said Stace and I went to line up with the other red setters in the ring. Merlot was young and lively and wanted to play with the other dogs. The other dogs were standing perfectly and the judge had started to make her rounds. I love showing dogs and felt quite excited to be doing this class. The standard was very high and all the owners looked very professional with their dogs being shown.

There were 8 dogs in our class. The judge was looking at Merlot. The judge asked if I could move the dog and I set off at a steady trot across the ring with Merlot gracefully showing off. The judge then wanted to look at the dogs' teeth. She started with Merlot. Merlot was a professional show dog and was used to having her teeth looked at often. All of a sudden one of the vintage motorbikes backfired and the noise frightened Merlot and she was off. She ran to the next ring which was the husky class. She raced along the line of huskies who were all standing beautifully. She barged into the first husky and he fell over. With that, the line of huskies all fell over one by one like a pack of cards. It was just so funny – but not to the owners of the huskies. Now the huskies had been released from their stand, they went to visit the Afghan hounds in the ring next to them.

The Afghan hounds were groomed to within an inch of their lives. But if a game was going on, then they wanted to be part of it. The immaculate hounds rolled on their backs on the show floor which was mainly made up of loose grass and sawdust.

Merlot was thoroughly enjoying her day out and was playing with a big husky running all over the floor and getting dirty and dusty. Showing had never been fun like this before!

Stace was going bananas and shouting to "get my Merlot back". I was shouting to people to catch her. After 15 minutes of madness, I managed to get Merlot back in the ring. All the red setters lined up again. The judge came over to me and presented us with a blue rosette for Second prize. She said to me that if my dog hadn't run off and caused such chaos then we would have had a first! The other owners in our class were disgusted by the whole episode and none of them congratulated us on the way out of the ring!

Pie and Mash

Also, at the Village Show was big Baz who was a regular. He was a gangster type and drove a black Range Rover with blacked out windows. He had two wonderful British bulldogs. Pie was the boy and his sister was Mash. They were so sturdy and had great personalities. Baz would drive them around in his car and they would make an entrance wherever they went.

Baz would take his sturdy dogs to the local agility classes. A British bulldog is not the usual dog for a bit of agility but a bulldog will not do anything unless there is something in it for them, but Baz thought they would be able to improve and liked to take them out to shows.

Mash wasn't interested in running around and going through tunnels as she was a bit of a prima donna but Pie wasn't proud and liked the treat of a sausage that he got at the end of it. They were the only bulldogs in the class and the sleek and intelligent collies who were there would eye the stout pair with disdain. The collies were always the best at this and knew they had it in the bag.

Baz was heavy and sturdy like his dogs so it was quite funny to watch as Baz lumbered up to the weaving poles with Pie and tell him to "get on with it mate"! Poor old Pie got stuck in the weaving poles and wouldn't move. Baz got a sausage out of his pocket to tempt Pie to carry on, but he gave the dog the sausage before it got to the end of the poles so it ate the sausage and still stood there. Next was the tunnel, which Pie liked. He liked to hide in the tunnel and it gave him a break. Pie ran into the tunnel and got stuck! Again, the collies looked at Big Baz as if to say he had no idea!

Luckily for Pie there was a sausage eating contest on next. Pie always did very well at this and ate all the other dog's sausages too. This was a class that Mash enjoyed too as she could eat lots of sausages and it didn't involve any agility. The bulldogs were not very popular as they had scoffed most of the sausages, leaving only a few for the other dogs. The posh lady judge came across and told Baz to remove "those fat greedy dogs from the ring".

With that Baz took his two dogs to have a rest in the shade. There was a car parked under a tree and one of the elderly lady judges was in the passenger side fast asleep snoring loudly. She had been helping herself to the bottle stall, which was next to her car. These were raffle prizes and had been called out by the elderly lady judge earlier. After a while the lady judge woke up and announced he winning raffle numbers. Lucky Baz won a box of dog biscuits and a bottle of champagne. So, all was not lost. The bulldogs had to be encouraged to walk back to the car and Pie just laid on his back with his legs in the air – full of sausages. The local farmer came along with his tractor and trailer giving the children rides and asked if Pie and Mash would like a lift back to the car. Both Pie and Mash were put on the trailer and taken back to the car park.

Both dogs were put in the Range Rover where they stayed for the hour's drive. All this agility was exhausting.

A plague of locusts

At the other end of the scale I have looked after bearded dragons who have very poor eyesight. I have had to pick up a wriggling locust with long tweezers and put the locust right up against the dragon's nose so it would be aware that food is there. Then a long tongue flicks out to catch the tasty treat. I had no experience with these lizards but thought as they were so slow and asleep most of the time it would be okay.

The locusts were kept in a Tupperware container in a drawer in the bedroom, next to the bearded dragon, together with meal worms, so I had to be really quick and careful about closing the drawer to stop the winged snacks escaping. Once I wasn't quick enough and the drawer was open for a few seconds too long. The locusts swarmed out of the drawer and were flying around the bedroom. It was impossible to catch them, so I had no choice but to open the window and wave goodbye to them. At least I had given them a brighter future!

A dog's Christmas shopping

I had a wonderful job once when I worked in the City before my pet sitting started. I worked for a barrister who had a lovely brown Labrador called Teddy who would come to work with him. I had the job of walking Teddy round the chambers. There was one incident where I had to chase Teddy as he did a runner with his owner's Court wig, but luckily his owner didn't notice even though one of the curls stuck out in a very cockatoo-esque manner afterwards! Teddy was the baby of the family and would often get treated as such.

I was typing up some notes when the barrister came out to see me with Teddy. Teddy always bought his "mother", the barrister's wife, - a Christmas present. The barrister asked if I could go with Teddy and the barrister's personal driver to the West End of London and help him spend his money. I was given a credit card and told to get Teddy's mother something very special and to also get myself something for my troubles.

This was a wonderful job that I was very happy to accept. It was also good to get out of the office for the afternoon. Teddy was not allowed in the posh West End shops so I went in on his behalf whilst he stayed in the plush town car with his head lolling out of the window and his tinsel decorations on and tried to catch passing shoppers with a lick.

I chose a Tiffany paw print necklace for Teddy's mother. I had such a wonderful afternoon and I got paid for it too – Teddy also treated me to a bottle of Chanel Number 5 perfume. What a good boy!

Thieving beagles

I love a beagle - they are such naughty dogs with an overdose of character, and just so funny. A lady I worked for called June, was having a lunch for a few friends and she had invited me to say thank you for walking her beagles. June had a very old mansion house with a big paddock at the back. June's husband Henry used to be a Master of Hounds for the local hunt. He retired years ago but still liked to keep up the discipline with his "pack" of two beagles.

When I arrived, the scene could not have been more idyllic. The weather was picture perfect and the magnificently decorated table was set out just next to the paddock. There were 12 of us. Some of the other guests had also brought their dogs to the lunch as June loved to welcome new canines to socialise with their pack.

Everyone was sitting round the table making polite conversation.

Henry came striding out wearing his hunting outfit complete with his hunting horn. We could all start eating when and only when the horn was blown. Discipline is always important and Henry said that sloppy ways would soon set in otherwise. So, we were all poised to dig in and help ourselves to the wonderful spread in front of us. I was hungry but sat there waiting like I was at school and doing what I was told. Henry didn't even get the chance to blow the horn. So, we were all sitting poised and ready.

All of a sudden, I saw a ginger and white flash as a beagle came flying across the table at speed and picked up not one but two daintily sliced smoked salmon slices from the bone china plate and ran off to the paddock with them. It was absolutely hilarious and certainly broke the ice with all he guests. Henry was going ballistic and blowing his horn at the beagle. Lack of discipline is a terrible thing and he would never stand for it in the olden days let alone now that he had more time for training. The next thing I knew - was a beagle assault from the other side of the table. The second beagle managed to scoop up a mouthful of prawns from a big salad dish. She then dropped the prawns on the grass and rolled on them to make sure they were dead before wolfing them down. The wonderful meal was going downhill quickly and order had to be restored. Henry was running about blasting on the horn and the beagles were helping themselves. They were too quick and too clever to be caught.

The other normal untrained dogs had been perfectly still watching the commotion. But the temptation was too much and the pointers joined in. It took about five full minutes for all the food to be snatched off the table.

The house used to be a court house in days gone by and there were cells at the back. Henry did no more but took all the naughty dogs away from the party and they were put in the cells until they could learn some manners and not do any more damage. That would be a while then.

It was such a funny experience and one which I will always remember!

James Pond – Sky Fool

.

I had a text message from a man called James. He had two male Labradors who were very strong and needed a couple of walks a day. He asked if I could come and meet the "boys". He said his wife, Minnie would be in during the day but he would like to make an appointment so he could meet me as well. I called ahead and said I would come up in the early evening.

I took my booking form and drove up to the hamlet where they lived. The address was number 7, Dark Lane.

A lady answered the door and said that her husband was delayed but would be back within the next 10 minutes. She offered me coffee which I accepted as I had been out all day walking dogs and it was good to sit down for a while.

She said she was called Minnie. There were two big Labradors asleep in their beds. They didn't even wake up with all that noise from the doorbell.

Minnie said her husband was called James and he had a successful swimming pool design business which he ran from the City. I immediately thought of his name James and could imagine he could be called James Pond 007 –

which made me laugh. She could be called Minnie Penny! I had to try and calm down a bit and act normally as I had just started my visit with them.

I was drinking my coffee and having a chat to Minnie. She was unhappy as she said James was always working late and she thought he was having an affair with his glamorous secretary. Minnie said she had never been glamorous but she kept the house running smoothly and said James didn't know how lucky he was. She said James loved himself and thought he was something. Well, I was shortly to meet that Something!

The coffee was so hot and I could only sip it slowly. This would take a while.

About 10 minutes later I heard the front door open. A man in his mid 30s, came striding towards me. He had sun-streaked hair which of which I was quite jealous! His looked natural and I had to pay for my highlights.

He winked at me and held out his hand – saying "Sorry I was late – got a bit held up". He indeed did seem to like himself not a bit but quite a whole lot. He was fascinating to watch and I had to keep my mind on my form and the job.

"Now then", said James – the boys must be woken up to meet you. "Spectre", "Oddjob" he yelled. The big dogs came lumbering over to lick his hand and I said hello to them as well.

Minnie said "I can't walk the boys – they are a bit too strong for me. I had walked Labradors before and owned them too, so I knew they could pull on the lead.

James had been staring at himself in the mirror and reminded me of a budgie preening. I wanted to say "who's a pretty boy then?" but stopped myself.

James suggested I took out the dogs to see if I could handle them. He put tracking devices on their leads and gave one to me too. I couldn't even ask about this as laughter was taking me over again. I hoped they wouldn't need the tracking devices and would stay with me.

I turned off the road to go around the fields. The dogs were sniffing and walking along slowly but were no trouble.

Ahead was a farmer driving a tractor. He saw me and called to the boys. The dogs took off like a Moonraker rocket (in my mind I was still playing the James Bond theme) and it was all I could do to hang on to their leads. The farmer got out a pack of digestive biscuits and gave them one each.

"Hello dear" he said – "I know these dogs – they belong to the blond bloke at number 7. "Are you the new dog walker then?". I had a few minutes more chat with the farmer and then headed back.

"Did you see that bloke on his tractor"? James asked. "Well I saw a farmer and he gave the boys a biscuit each". "He's just trying to get them to talk – said James. Been at it for years and they haven't given in – even for a biscuit, as they are highly trained field agents"

James went back to the mirror in the hall way and blew kisses at himself. The mirror was smeared and cloudy and I reckoned he really did actually kiss the mirror when everyone was out.

Minnie told me "he loves himself". I silently agreed there. The next thing was almost unbelievable. Minnie went over to James and pulled down his trousers. She said to me "look – he even has his union jack boxer shorts on"!

This was the start of a whole new mission for me.

I left the coffee and went out to my car – laughing hysterically and shaken not stirred!

Caught on camera

I had a lovely job in a big Tudor country house. I had to look after three little white poodles as a regular booking. They all had pink diamante collars and were called Frankie, Fifi and Fofo - try saying that three times fast across the park! Their owners were really nice people and would fly off on holiday for a couple of weeks and I would move into one of the spare rooms upstairs to stay with the dogs. There was also a big pond full of koi carp and 6 ducks to look after. I loved the job and the grounds were so big, I could walk round them and still get lost on the way back to the house.

The house itself was massive and beautifully decorated with a cinema room where I spent a lot of time. There were cameras all around the front and back gardens and there were six screens in the kitchen alone where I could keep an eye out that everything was as it should be.

Those screens made me a bit paranoid though and I kept imagining all the horror movies I had ever seen and especially the one with the mask from the Scream movies. I kept checking the screens, especially at night. I didn't get much sleep as I felt I couldn't fully relax. The dogs would start barking and scratching around at night and they just sat and stared at the front door all in a row. I managed to quieten them down but they kept running back to the door.

One night I went to bed and then was woken up to hear the dogs barking again. I went to turn on the light but nothing. We were having a power cut or so I thought, or indeed, this was the latest horror film scene and the guy in the Scream mask would be phoning at any moment demanding "what's your favourite scary movie". I decided if he did phone, I wouldn't tell him!

This was my worst nightmare, as I would have to now ring the owner - Justin - and find out where the electrical switches were. I went downstairs in my nightie (I should really start wearing pyjamas, I don't have much luck in nighties!) - luckily it was summer so not at all cold. I saw that both the freezers and the fridges in the kitchen had gone off.

I rang the owner and he told me I would have to go outside and open the garage door with a remote control. I did this and had to clamber on two plastic chairs stacked together while still trying to hold my mobile phone to my ear for instructions in order to turn the power back on. It was not a power cut but the circuit had blown a fuse and I would have to flick the switch to put the power back on again.

I tottered about on my perch of two chairs and managed with the help of a broom handle to reach the switch and turn it on again.

This done, I went to the garage door to get out but as I was half way out and the garage door came down on my shoulder and pinned me against the dustbin. I was stuck in the middle of the night half in and half out of the garage in my nightie with a broomstick! The three little dogs were barking like mad as to them this was highly irregular to be out in the garden with me in the middle of the night, they must have thought they were going out for a walk.

I was also caught on the security cameras which were linked up to the police station. I didn't know this and the owner had not told me. So, here I was in the early hours of the morning, making myself a coffee and trying to settle the dogs down, when a knock came at the door which scared the living daylights out of me. A voice said "open up – police". I opened the door with caution and there stood two police officers. They came in and had a coffee with me and we all had a big laugh about it all. This was one night I would not forget!

When I went back to the house three weeks later to return the key and collect my money, the lovely owner Justin had the biggest box of chocolates for me to say thank you but he had also bought me a new M&S nightie and said on the film from the cameras it looked as though I needed a new one!

As I did more jobs I started walking faster and further. Some of the dogs were very young and lively so I had to keep up with them. I would space out my jobs so after a couple of hours' walking, I would fit in a cat sitting job. A few of my customers would want me to sit with the animals and keep them company. They would leave me out a cup and some biscuits so I could make myself a coffee and sit down to watch the latest episode of Judge Rinder! It was good to be able to have a break after the rushing around.

I also had some elderly dogs that just needed 5 minutes in the garden and then they would come and sit next to me for an hour. People just liked the day to be broken up for the animals.

Some of my jobs were at the opposite of the scale and I had lively dogs who definitely did not want to sit down with me for an hour. It was with these dogs I needed more energy. I took a husky out walking but he didn't want to walk but wanted to run!

Since becoming a pet sitter I have had fun, met some great people (and many strange ones) and their animals. It all adds to the variety of my days. I do not miss being a legal secretary one little bit.

But the main thing is, they are always pleased to see me and happy with the attention.

Biography

I am a 62 year old pet sitter. I started pet sitting just to help my daughter out. I am a retired legal secretary and love dogs and cats - especially as they are always in a good mood and do not answer back. A refreshing change from some of the lawyers I worked for!

My stories are from real experiences I have had since I started this. I always have something to talk about when I meet the owners of the pets. But for one thing it is never boring and never predictable!

Helen Brunton

Printed in Great Britain
by Amazon

46148563R00078